Science and Technology for Children BOOKS™

Animal Studies

JESSIE COHEN, NATIONAL ZOOLOGICAL PARK, SMITHSONIAN INSTITUTION

National Science Resources Center

THE NATIONAL ACADEMIES Smithsonian Institution

National Science Resources Center
The establishment of the National Science Resources Center (NSRC) by two of the nation's most prestigious institutions, the Smithsonian Institution and the National Academies, provides the United States with a unique resource for catalyzing change in science education. The NSRC is an organization of the Smithsonian Institution and the National Academies; its mission is to improve the learning and teaching of science in the nation's school districts. The NSRC disseminates information about exemplary teaching resources, develops curriculum materials, and conducts outreach programs of leadership development, technical assistance, and professional development to help school districts implement research based science education programs for all K–12 students.

Smithsonian Institution
One of the NSRC's parent organizations is the Smithsonian Institution. The Smithsonian Institution was created by an act of Congress in 1846 "for the increase and diffusion of knowledge...." This independent federal establishment is the world's largest museum complex and is responsible for public and scholarly activities, exhibitions, and research projects nationwide and overseas. Among the objectives of the Smithsonian is the application of its unique resources to enhance elementary and secondary education.

The National Academies
The National Academies are also a parent organization of the NSRC. The National Academies are nonprofit organizations that provide independent advice to the nation on matters of science, technology, and medicine. The National Academies consist of four organizations: the National Academy of Sciences, the National Academy of Engineering, the Institute of Medicine, and the National Research Council. The National Academy of Sciences was created in 1863 by a congressional charter. Under this charter, the National Research Council was established in 1916, the National Academy of Engineering in 1964, and the Institute of Medicine in 1970.

Acknowledgments

Animal Studies is part of a series of books for students in kindergarten through sixth grade, and it is an integral part of the Science and Technology for Children® (STC®) curriculum program. The purpose of these books is to enhance and extend STC's inquiry-based investigations through reading. Research has shown that students improve their reading skills when challenged with interesting and engaging reading materials. In the process, key science concepts that students have been learning can be reinforced. The Teacher's Guide that accompanies the STC program gives some information on how to integrate this book with the program's inquiry-centered investigations. Those students interested in reading these books on their own will find them easy to read as stand-alone texts. All students will especially enjoy reading about highlights of the Smithsonian Institution's varied and unique museums.

The book has undergone rigorous review by experts in the field to ensure that all the information is current and accurate. A nationally recognized reading specialist has worked with us to create stories that are at a reading level that is appropriate for students in fourth and fifth grades. We have also varied the reading level throughout the book so that all students—no matter what their reading proficiency—can find stories that are both interesting and challenging.

The NSRC greatly appreciates the efforts of all the individuals listed below. Each contributed his or her expertise to ensure that the book is of the highest quality.

Science and Technology for Children Books: *Animal Studies*

National Science Resources Center Staff and Consultants

Sally Goetz Shuler
Executive Director

Marilyn Fenichel
Managing Editor (consultant)

Linda Harteker
Senior Editor (consultant)

Heather Dittbrenner
Copy Editor (consultant)

Gail Peck
Designer (consultant)

Heidi M. Kupke
Graphic Designer

Max-Karl Winkler
Illustrator

Christine Hauser
Photo Editor

Susan Tannahill
Webmaster and Database Specialist

Kimberly Wayman
Procurement and Financial Assistant

Research and Development Staff and Advisors

David Marsland
Co-Director, Professional Development Center
NSRC

Henry Milne
Co-Director, Professional Development Center
NSRC

Carole C. Baldwin
Research Zoologist
National Museum of Natural History
Smithsonian Institution
Washington, DC

Jonathan Ballou
Director, Behavior and Ecology Division
National Zoological Park
Smithsonian Institution
Washington, DC

Kimbra Cutlip
Education and Outreach
Smithsonian Environmental Research Center
Edgewater, MD

Brian A. Hazlett
Department of Biology
University of Michigan
Ann Arbor, MI

Anson H. Hines, Jr.
Assistant Director
Environmental Biology
Smithsonian Environmental Research Center
Edgewater, MD

Peter Marra
Senior Scientist
Smithsonian Environmental Research Center
Edgewater, MD

Lynne Murdock
Natural Resource Interpretive Specialist
National Park Service
Washington, DC

David Pawson
Senior Research Zoologist
National Museum of Natural History
Smithsonian Institution
Washington DC

Roger Rosscoe
Animal Keeper
National Zoological Park
Smithsonian Institution
Washington, DC

Robert W. Shumaker
Biologist
National Zoological Park
Smithsonian Institution
Washington, DC

Carla Truax
Education Specialist
Center for Global Environmental Education
St. Paul, MN

Annemarie Sullivan Palincsar
Jean and Charles Walgreen Professor of Reading and Literacy
School of Education
University of Michigan
Ann Arbor, MI

Ian MacGregor
President
Science Education Associates
Berkeley, CA

Judith White
Curriculum Developer
STC Discovery Decks
Berkeley, CA

Carolina Biological Supply Company Staff

Dianne Gerlach
Director of Product Development

David Heller
Department Head, Product Development

Robert Mize
Department Head, Publications

Jennifer Manske
Publications Manager

Gary Metheny
Editor

Cindy Morgan
Senior Curriculum Product Manager

This book is one of a series that has been designed to be an integral component of the Science and Technology for Children® curriculum, an innovative, hands-on science program for children in grades kindergarten through six. This program would not have been possible without the generous support of federal agencies, private foundations, and corporations. Supporters include the National Science Foundation, the Smithsonian Institution, the U.S. Department of Defense, the U.S. Department of Education, the John D. and Catherine T. MacArthur Foundation, the Dow Chemical Company Foundation, the Amoco Foundation, Inc., DuPont, the Hewlett-Packard Company, the Smithsonian Institution Educational Outreach Fund, and the Smithsonian Women's Committee.

© 2004 The National Academy of Sciences and the Smithsonian Institution

09 08   10 9 8 7 6 5 4 3

ISBN 978-1-933008-00-4

All rights reserved. No part of this book may be reproduced or utilized in any form or by any means, electronic or mechanical, including photocopying, recording, or by any other storage and retrieval system without permission in writing from the National Science Resources Center, except for the purposes of official use by the U.S. government. Contact www.nsrconline.org for further information.

Science and Technology for Children BOOKS™

Animal Studies

CONTENTS

Introduction 4

PART 1:
Animals and Where They Live

Frogs, Toads, and Other Amphibians 6
A Crab's Life 9
A Close Look at Birds 12
What Makes Beavers Special? 16
Conclusion 20

p. 16

PART 2:
Animal Behavior

Cat and Dog Talk 22
Animal Signs 26
How Do Hermit Crabs Find New Shells? 30
Conclusion 33

p. 30

PART 3:
Keeping Animals Safe

Animal Keeper 35
What Happened to the Frogs? 38
Going Home Again 40
Conclusion 43

p. 38

PART 4:
Scientists at Work

The Amazing Discoveries of Charles Darwin 45
Jean-Henri Fabré: Science Pioneer 50
Orangutans and How They Learn 53
The Story of Konrad Lorenz 56
Jane Goodall and Her Life with the Chimps 58
Conclusion 62

Glossary 63

p. 52

ABOVE—FROG MISSING A LEG: COURTESY OF MINNESOTA POLLUTION CONTROL AGENCY, ST. PAUL, MN; MONARCH BUTTERFLY: COURTESY OF CAROLINA BIOLOGICAL SUPPLY COMPANY
COVER—ORANGUTAN MALE PORTRAIT: JESSIE COHEN, NATIONAL ZOOLOGICAL PARK, SMITHSONIAN INSTITUTION; AMERICAN TOAD: COURTESY OF CAROLINA BIOLOGICAL SUPPLY COMPANY; BLUE JAY: JESSIE COHEN, NATIONAL ZOOLOGICAL PARK, SMITHSONIAN INSTITUTION; HERMIT CRAB: JESSIE COHEN, NATIONAL ZOOLOGICAL PARK, SMITHSONIAN INSTITUTION

Introduction

Our world is full of animals. They live everywhere on Earth, from the hottest desert to the deep freeze of the polar regions. Animals also live in every environment imaginable—on land, in the deep ocean, on the tops of trees, and in the soil.

Animals are as different as the places in which they live. Some are big, while others are too small to see with your eyes alone. Some animals are covered with fur, while others have rough, bumpy skin or a skeleton covering their body. Most birds, of course, are covered with feathers.

Although animals are very different, they also are alike in many important ways. All animals need food, water, air, and shelter.

For some animals, taking care of all their needs is sometimes difficult. For one thing, they live in an environment with many other animals. All the animals are looking for food and and water, and some animals are food, or prey, for other animals. That means that animals also must be able to protect themselves from their enemies.

How do animals survive in their environment? Animals' bodies and behaviors have characteristics that enable them to meet their basic needs. These characteristics are called adaptations.

THIS BOOK IS ABOUT ANIMALS AND THEIR ADAPTATIONS TO THEIR ENVIRONMENT. You will discover how some of these adaptations are physical characteristics, such as their outer coverings or the shape of their bodies. But you also will read about many adaptations that involve what animals do in their environment. These actions, or behaviors, include how animals find food and avoid enemies. These behaviors help animals survive.

We know about animals because scientists study them. This book includes stories about different kinds of scientists and the techniques they use to learn about animals. You will also find out about scientists who paved the way for many of our important discoveries about animals.

As you read these stories, think about the animals in your own environment. How do they find food? How do they escape from their enemies? What behaviors help them survive?

 *If you see this icon in the upper right-hand corner, it's a story about scientists and the work they do.*

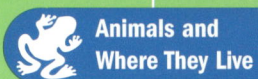

PART 1

ANIMALS AND WHERE THEY LIVE

The four stories in Part 1 are the following:

- Frogs, Toads, and Other Amphibians
- A Crab's Life
- A Close Look at Birds
- What Makes Beavers Special?

They focus on how animals are adapted to their environment. It's amazing how well suited many animals are to the places where they live.

You'll also see what can happen when the environment changes, often leaving animals with no place to live.

You will also discover an animal that can change its environment. This animal is not a human being either. Do you know what animal it is? If not, read on and find out.

SMITHSONIAN ENVIRONMENTAL RESEARCH CENTER

ANIMAL STUDIES • STC BOOKS   5

Frogs, Toads, and Other Amphibians

A fire salamander

Frog's eggs

Frogs and toads belong to a group of animals called amphibians. The word amphibian tells you something interesting about these animals. "Amphi" means "both" in Greek. Adult amphibians lay their eggs in the water but spend most of their time on land, near water. Developing lungs and living their adult life on land is an important adaptation for amphibians.

About 2,600 different kinds of amphibians live on Earth. They're found all over the world, except in very cold places. Usually, they live in moist areas so that their skin will not dry out.

About 2,600 different kinds of amphibians live on earth.

Giant Toad

Ways Amphibians Are Alike

All amphibians share some key characteristics. This list explains two ways that amphibians are alike.

◆ Female amphibians lay eggs in water or in moist places. Their eggs are different from hens' eggs. They don't have shells. Without water, the eggs would dry out. Then the babies inside would die.

◆ Amphibian young are called larvae. Larvae do not look like adults when they hatch out of the eggs. They must go through several physical changes. These changes are known as metamorphosis. During metamorphosis, amphibians lose their gills and develop lungs. Why is that change an important adaptation? Animals use gills to breathe in the water and lungs to breathe on land.

Think about where amphibians spend most of their adult lives. Then it will be easy to answer the question.

A Closer Look at Two Amphibians

Frogs and toads are two common amphibians. At first glance, people may think they look alike. But frogs and toads are really quite different.

Look closely at the two pictures on this page. Pay attention to each animal's skin, body shape, legs, and feet. How do you think frogs and toads are different? How are they alike? Make your own list before reading on.

Differences between Frogs and Toads

◆ Most frogs, like the one shown at left, have smooth, wet skin. Toads, shown above, have rough, bumpy, skin. Their skin is also pretty dry.

◆ The back legs of frogs are much bigger than the front legs. Many ▶

Bullfrog

ANIMAL STUDIES ● STC BOOKS   7

kinds of frogs, such as bullfrogs, have a lot of webbing between their toes. The webbing helps bullfrogs move quickly in the water. Why is the ability to move fast an important adaptation for bullfrogs?

- The front and hind legs of toads are just about the same length. They have a little bit of webbing between their toes.

- Toads live in much dryer places than frogs do. Toads walk a lot, while frogs mostly hop or jump. Frogs' long, powerful hind legs make them excellent leapers, too.

Now you know how frogs and toads are different. How are they similar? Look at the list at the beginning of the story before answering. Those are the main ways that frogs and toads are alike.

Here's another similarity: Some toads have large skin glands. These glands have poison inside them. The poison helps protect the toad from its enemies. Some frogs, such as the poison arrow frog, also have poison. Be sure to wash your hands after you touch a toad or a frog.

Other Kinds of Amphibians

Frogs and toads are examples of only two kinds of amphibians. There are many more. Here's a peek at a couple of other amphibians.

SALAMANDERS. Salamanders have long tails and four short legs. Salamanders use their tails for swimming. There are more than 400 kinds of salamanders. They live in Asia, Europe, and North America. Like frogs and toads, salamanders go through metamorphosis. During this process they, too, lose their gills and develop lungs.

CAECILIANS. A caecilian is a small, skinny amphibian. A caecilian looks a little like a worm. It has no limbs at all. There are more than 150 kinds of caecilians. Most people have never seen one. That's because they hide under moist leaves or damp soil. They also live far away, in the tropical forests of South America and Asia.

Think about what you just learned about amphibians. Try to remember two adaptations. Discuss them with your friends. Make a list of the ways that amphibians are well suited to their environment.

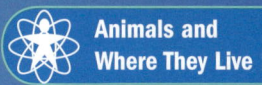
Animals and Where They Live

A Crab's Life

Have you ever eaten a Chesapeake Bay blue crab?

Lots of people have eaten crabs. Fish like to eat them, too. In fact, its scientific name, *Callinectus sapidus*, means "beautiful swimmer that tastes good." That's not so good if you're a blue crab.

Lucky for the crabs, scientists are interested in doing more than just eating them. They want to learn all that they can about the blue crab. Researcher Anson "Tuck" Hines and other scientists at the Smithsonian Environmental Research Center (SERC) in Edgewater, Maryland, are studying crabs.

ANIMAL STUDIES • STC BOOKS

A blue crab with instruments on different parts of its body.

They began their research with a number of questions:

? What do crabs do all day?

? What do crabs eat?

? How long does it take for crabs to eat one meal?

? How do young crabs protect themselves from their enemies?

To answer these questions, they observed crabs very closely for long periods of time. However, because crabs live in muddy water, they are very hard to see. The scientists needed tools to help them. They attached small instruments to the crabs. The instruments send signals through the water. Using special equipment, Tuck can pick up the signals and listen to them on his headphones.

Over the years, Tuck and his team of scientists have tracked hundreds of crabs. They figured out that they could put the very tiny instruments in different places on the crab's body. Each instrument gave off a different kind of beep. Each beep let scientists know what the crabs were doing. Tuck and his team could then answer their questions about crabs.

Here's what the scientists found out.

WHAT DO CRABS DO ALL DAY? Crabs spend a lot of time searching for food and fighting each other.

Tuck Hines listens for "beeps" from the instruments while another scientist observes the crab.

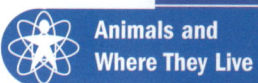
Animals and Where They Live

> Something else has happened to blue crabs. People have changed the crabs' environment, and they have not been able to adapt.

WHAT DO CRABS EAT? They like to eat clams. But if there are no clams around, they will eat each other. That's why they fight so much.

HOW LONG DOES IT TAKE FOR CRABS TO EAT ONE MEAL? Crabs eat for a long time. Sometimes, they may eat for a few hours. At other times, they can eat for a few days.

HOW DO YOUNG CRABS PROTECT THEMSELVES FROM THEIR ENEMIES? They hide in marsh grasses. If people cut the marsh grass, the crabs have trouble hiding. That's why it's important to preserve the marsh grasses.

Crabs in Trouble

Scientists need the information they have gathered about blue crabs. It helps them understand what is happening to blue crabs. Blue crabs are in trouble, and it's not just because they are eaten a lot.

Something else has happened to the blue crab. People have changed their environment, and the blue crabs have not been able to adapt. Here are three ways that their environment has been changed.

- Pollution in the Bay has killed the grasses along the shore. That is bad news for the crabs. Now they have no place to hide from all the fish and other predators that want to eat them. They are easier to find, so more crabs get eaten.

- People have built houses, hotels, restaurants, and other businesses along the Chesapeake Bay. When clearing, workers removed dead trees and rocks. Dead trees and rocks are good hiding places for crabs. When they're taken away, crabs have fewer places to go.

- People have taken too many crabs out of the Bay. Now there are barely enough adult crabs to produce baby crabs. As a result, the crab population has gone down.

Now that you know why blue crabs are in trouble, what can humans do to help? Begin by thinking about what has happened to their environment. What can we do to make it more like it used to be? Be sure to share your ideas with adults. They can work with you to help the Chesapeake Bay blue crab survive. ■

ANIMAL STUDIES • STC BOOKS

A Close Look at Birds

Many people love watching birds just for the joy of it. But some people study birds closely for another very important reason. They want to understand how changes in a bird's environment affect it.

Animals and Where They Live

Scientists know that the environments of many birds in Maryland are changing. They also know that the numbers of some birds are dropping. They are trying to figure out if changes in the environment are causing the changes in the numbers of birds in Maryland.

But scientists can't do this work alone. They need your help. That's why researchers at the Smithsonian Environmental Research Center (SERC), in Edgewater, Maryland, are teaching amateur birdwatchers how to study birds. They are part of a program called Neighborhood Nestwatch. The program was started by an ecologist named Dr. Peter Marra. While this program is just for birdwatchers in Maryland, there may be other programs like it near where you live. If you're interested, check them out.

Here's how Neighborhood Nestwatch works.

Interested participants choose a bird they often see in their own backyard. Then a scientist from the Nestwatch program will visit the birdwatcher's home. The participants point out the bird they have chosen. It may be a cardinal because these bright red birds are easy to see. Or people may be interested in watching robins or mockingbirds. After the bird has been chosen, the researcher puts up a special net so that the bird can be caught safely.

After catching the bird, scientists perform the following tests:

1. First, they measure the bird's beak from the tip to where it meets the bird's head. The beak size gives information

The bird's wing is being measured.

about the health of the bird. They use a tool called a ruler and calipers. The tool is shown here, and it is being used to measure the length of the bird's wing. ▸

ANIMAL STUDIES • STC BOOKS 13

Did you know that some birds appear to be a different color when they are flying than when they are not flying?

2. Next, they weigh the bird by putting it in a special bird bag. Putting the bird in the bag doesn't hurt it. In fact, the bag helps calm the bird down. When the bird is ready, the scientist weighs the bird—in its bag—on a spring scale. Do you think weighing the bird in the bag is going to give the right weight of the bird? If you said no, you're right. The researcher must weigh the bag first and then subtract its weight from the total. What's left is the weight of the bird.

3. Finally, the scientist must put a band on the bird. Birds being watched wear four bands. One is an aluminum band. The aluminum band will let people anywhere in the world know that this bird has been studied. The other three bands are colored. The unique band combination is like the bird's "name." It lets both amateur and professional birdwatchers pick out the bird year after year.

After the researcher has taken the measurements, the bird is released. But the birdwatcher's job is not done. Now it's time to look for the bird's nest. If the birdwatchers find it, they write down where it is located. A nest is a good sign. It means that the bird is doing well in its neighborhood. It is able to take care of its young, raising a new generation of birds.

In Your Own Backyard

You can become a birdwatcher, too. Start collecting information about birds in your neighborhood. Notice which birds you

This bird is being "banded."

14 ANIMAL STUDIES • STC BOOKS

Animals and Where They Live

Birdwatchers may see different kinds of beaks like these. Why do birds have different-shaped beaks?

see at different times of the year. If possible, use binoculars. Buy a field guide so you can figure out which birds they are. Pay close attention to what the birds are doing.

Some birds you see stay in one area all year long. Others migrate in the winter. That means they fly many miles every year from their spring and summer homes to their winter homes. Many of these birds have their babies in their spring and summer homes.

When you spot a bird, you should stay at least $4\frac{1}{2}$ meters, about 15 feet, away. Move as slowly and quietly as possible. The quieter you are, the more likely the bird will continue behaving naturally.

In the spring, you may see a bird carrying a twig or bit of string. This means it's building a nest nearby. If you follow the bird, you may be able to watch it work. Among some types of birds, the males and females both build nests. Among others, only the female builds the nest. Among still others, the male builds a nest to attract a mate. Once a bird finds a

spot it likes, it can build a nest in three to five days.

While birdwatching, you may see one bird chasing another. You may wonder why. Are they fighting over food, or is one protecting a nest? Watch and try to find out.

If you watch long enough, you'll discover just how much is going on in your own backyard. ■

ANIMAL STUDIES ● STC BOOKS   15

What Makes Beavers Special?

Look! Over there! An animal is holding a branch in its mouth. What animal do you think it is? What is the animal going to do with the branch?

THIS IS A BEAVER IN ITS HABITAT.
A habitat is a place where plants and animals live. Animals need food, water, air, and shelter. Every animal has characteristics that are just right for its habitat. Read on to find out how the beaver is able to live in its habitat. You may be surprised to learn how clever the beaver is.

Most animals must find a habitat that meets their needs. But the beaver is different. The beaver is a lot like us. It finds a habitat and then changes it to suit its needs.

The beaver changes the habitat by building a dam.

On Land and In Water

Beavers live on land and in water. On land, beavers are clumsy. Their front legs are short. They cannot walk very fast. On land, they have trouble escaping from their enemies. But in the water, beavers have an easier time. They are excellent swimmers and divers. They use their broad tails like a boat paddle to help them move through the water. They move quickly and gracefully in the water.

Wolves and bears are the beaver's enemies, or predators. These predators hunt and eat beavers. To keep its family safe, a beaver builds its home partly in the water. That home is called a lodge. The only way to get into the lodge is through an underwater tunnel.

Why Build a Dam?

But what if the river or stream is too shallow to build a lodge? Rather than search for a different site, the beaver will build a dam. A dam holds back the water. To build the dam, beavers use their front feet. They push mud, branches, and stones to create a ridge in the water. Then they use their sharp teeth to cut down trees.

Beavers cut down most of the trees near the water. Then they go into the woods for more trees. It is easier for beavers to move the heavy wood by floating it in water than by dragging it on land, so they dig canals in the ground. Water runs along the canals, which connect the wooded area to the pond. The beavers use the canals to float the logs down to the river.

This is a completed beaver lodge.

The beavers push the freshly cut sticks and logs into the muddy ridge they have created. Now the dam is complete. Water cannot flow easily above or around the dam. Soon the water in the stream forms a deep pond. Then the beaver can build its lodge.

Step Inside . . .

From the outside, a beaver's lodge looks like a pile of sticks in the water. But inside, the beavers are dry and cozy. Inside their home, they build ledges above the water. The beavers sleep on the ledges, which are made of sticks, wood chips, and grass.

Before winter comes, the beavers will add layers of sticks and mud to the lodge roof. The mud will harden and keep the lodge warm even in the coldest weather.

The beavers also collect extra sticks and leaves. These make a good food pile. Beavers keep the food pile in the water. They put it just below the tunnel that leads into the lodge. When the pond freezes, the beavers leave the lodge and swim to the bottom of the tunnel. They can eat from the food pile without ever leaving the water.

Keeping Warm and Dry

Like all mammals, beavers are warm-blooded. They also have fur. The outside layer of guard hairs is long and stiff. They protect the underfur, which is short and soft.

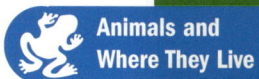
Animals and Where They Live

The underfur traps air to protect the beaver from the cold and to prevent water from reaching the skin. A layer of fat under the fur also helps keep the beaver warm.

A beaver also has glands that produce oil. The beaver puts the oil on its fur using a special "split toenail," located on the second toe of each back foot. The oil helps prevent the fur from absorbing water that can wet the beaver's skin.

Special Body Parts

A beaver has other special body structures that help it swim and work. Its back, or hind, feet are webbed like a duck's. The beaver's feet help it move through the water. The beaver's wide, flat tail helps it steer.

Beavers also use their tails to communicate. A beaver sniffs the air and listens. A fox is coming near. Whap! A beaver smacks its wide tail on the surface of the water. Do you know why? That slap is a warning sign. When other beavers hear it, they swim to the lodge for safety.

Beavers use their tails on land, too. The tail supports them like another leg. Beavers stand when they are cutting down trees. The tail helps them balance.

Like rats and squirrels, beavers are rodents, or gnawing mammals. A beaver has a hard orange coating on its two top and bottom front teeth. This coating keeps the teeth from chipping. The beaver has two folds of skin behind the front teeth. These folds keep water out of the beaver's mouth while it gnaws on wood under water.

Have you ever used goggles in a pool? A beaver has its own built-in goggles. Each eye has a clear inner eyelid. This eyelid covers and protects the beaver's eye so it can see under water.

Beavers can stay under water for up to 15 minutes! Their lungs can hold a great amount of air. A beaver also slows down its heart rate when it dives. That way, it uses less oxygen when under water. A valve in the beaver's nose closes the nostrils while it swims.

The beaver is well adapted to survive in its habitat. Like humans, beavers can change their environment to better meet their needs. ■

PART 1 **CONCLUSION**

Animals and Where They Live

I KNOW THAT ONE! It lays its eggs in the water and then spends most of its time on land, near water. What animal is it?

GOOD TO KNOW! During metamorphosis, amphibians lose their gills and develop lungs. Look up metamorphosis in the Glossary at the back of this book.

THAT'S EASY! Pollution in the Chesapeake Bay has killed marsh grasses along the shore. Why is this bad news for blue crabs?

THAT'S A FACT! Smithsonian scientists measure a bird's beak from the tip to where it meets the bird's head because the beak size gives information about the health of the bird.

WHAT DO YOU THINK? What distinguishes beavers from other animals?

PART 2
Animal Behavior

Animals lead busy lives. They must look for food and water, find shelter, protect themselves from enemies, and take care of their young. To complete these tasks, animals have developed interesting ways to communicate with one another—and with any humans in their lives. The stories discuss different kinds of animal behavior. Discover how clever animals really are. Pick up some tips on how to tell if animals have been nearby.

In Part 2, you will read these three stories:
- Cat and Dog Talk
- Animal Signs
- How Do Hermit Crabs Find New Shells?

Cat and Dog Talk

How Animals Communicate

Think about the many ways you communicate your thoughts and feelings. You use words but you also use your face, and your whole body. Now think about other animals. How do they communicate? Cats and dogs may not communicate with words, but they communicate in many other ways.

Cat Communication

Meow, meow! That's one way cats communicate. But cats also communicate with their bodies and their facial expressions. Head and tail position, ears, eyes, and whiskers can tell a lot about what a cat is feeling.

Postures

Neutral
The tail is held high, and is bent slightly forward.

Defensive
The tail is puffy and curls close to the body over the back.

Relaxed and Confident
The tail swishes freely behind the cat.

Aggressive
The tail puffs up and is dropped down. The cat's back is slightly arched.

Calling Cards

So far, we have learned about how cats communicate their feelings. Cats can communicate other information as well.

Why is this cat rubbing up against a post? She's leaving her *calling card*. That's a message, in the form of a scent that other cats can smell. The scent is made by an oily substance found in skin on the cat's chin, lips, temples, and at the base of its tail.

Facial Expressions

Here are some typical expressions you can expect to find on a cat's face.

Relaxed

The pupils are small, and the cat's ears and whiskers are down.

Annoyed

The pupils are small. The ears are turned back, and the whiskers are pushed forward.

Excited

The cat's pupils are large, and the ears are perked up.

Fearful

The pupils are large. The ears are flattened, and the whiskers are pulled back. ▸

ANIMAL STUDIES • STC BOOKS

Dog Dialogue

You certainly know that dogs bark. It's one way they communicate with you and other animals. But like cats, dogs have other ways to communicate. Dogs also express themselves through posture, facial expressions, and scent and marking.

Postures

Calm
The ears and tail are relaxed.

Alert
The ears and tail are up.

Aggressive
The hairs along the neck, called hackles, are up, along with the tail and the rump. The dog's lips are pulled back.

Afraid
The dog is crouched, with its tail between its legs.

Submissive
The dog is lying down, with its hind legs lifted.

Scent and Marking

Scent is probably a dog's most highly developed means of communication. Dogs communicate by smelling saliva, feces, urine, and tail glands. Dog feces and urine act like calling cards to other dogs, giving information about the sex, age, and size of the dog. Why do you think that male dogs lift their leg as high as possible when they urinate?

Facial Expressions

Neutral

This dog is not showing any strong emotions.

Attack

This dog's ears are forward and alert, its mouth is slightly open, and its hair bristles. The dog is very angry.

Submissive

This dog's ears and head are flattened out. It is ready to obey its owner.

Comparing Cat and Dog Talk

Now that you know a little bit about "cat and dog talk," think about these sets of behavior. How are they alike? How are they different? Do you think cats and dogs are successful in communicating their needs and feelings? ■

Animal Signs

Learn To Be a Zoologist

Have you ever heard of a scientist called a zoologist? If not, look closely at the word. You can see that it contains the word "zoo." That's a good hint. It tells you that a zoologist probably has something to do with animals. In fact, a zoologist is a scientist who studies animals.

Zoologists know of many ways to study animals. You can learn some of these ways, too. A good first step is to learn how to find animals by studying clues they leave behind.

Tracks

Animal tracks are one sign that an animal has been nearby. Look for tracks along the muddy edge of a

pond or on a sandy beach. Check the sides of country roads for animal tracks made in the dust. In winter, you may see tracks in the snow.

A good time to look for tracks is early in the morning. You may be able to see tracks left the night before.

More Signs

Near animal tracks, you can often find other clues—animal droppings. That may sound gross, but animal droppings are important animal signs. Did you know that the color,

26 ANIMAL STUDIES • STC BOOKS

shape, and texture of droppings vary among different animals? Many experienced animal watchers can identify animals by their droppings.

Animal droppings near a tree.

Now It's Your Turn

Can you figure out which animal is which from its tracks and droppings? Turn the page and try matching the animals to their signs. Think about what you know about the size and the weight of these animals.

If you become serious about tracking animals, you'll need a good field guide. There are lots to choose from. One is *A Field Guide to Mammals*, by William Henry Burt and Richard Philip Grossenheider. ▸

Children visiting a nature center point out raccoon tracks.

ANIMAL STUDIES • STC BOOKS 27

Play the Animal Matching Game

Match the animal to the signs. Don't look at the answers until you've tried them all.

- **WHITE-TAILED DEER**
- **STRIPED SKUNK**
- **NORWAY RAT**
- **RACCOON**
- **COTTONTAIL**
- **COYOTE**

28 ANIMAL STUDIES • STC BOOKS

D

E

F

ANSWERS
A. Striped skunk
B. White-tailed deer
C. Cottontail
D. Coyote
E. Norway rat
F. Raccoon

ANIMAL STUDIES • STC BOOKS   29

HOW DO Hermit Crabs FIND NEW SHELLS?

JESSIE COHEN, NATIONAL ZOOLOGICAL PARK, SMITHSONIAN INSTITUT

An animal peeks out from its home in a shell. This animal is called a hermit crab. It belongs to a larger group of animals called crustaceans. Other crustaceans include barnacles and shrimp. All crustaceans live in the water. Some live in fresh water, while others live in salt water.

Hermit crabs live in salt water near the shore.

Hermit crabs come in many different sizes. In fact, there are more than 600 kinds of hermit crabs. Some grow to be 30 cm (1 foot) long. Others are less than 2.5 cm (1 inch) long.

Unlike other crabs, hermit crabs have soft bellies. They need some way to protect this part of their bodies. The way that hermit crabs protect their bellies is a good example of an adaptation.

Are you ready to find out how hermit crabs protect their soft bellies? They use shells for protection. They crawl into empty snail shells they see on the beach. The shell becomes the crab's safe little house.

As the crab grows, it needs a larger shell. The crab also wants the most comfortable shell it can find. So hermit crabs are constantly looking for new shells.

Hermit crabs check out new shells to see if they would make a good home. (See page 32.)

What Kind of Shells Do Crabs Prefer?

Scientists were interested in finding out what kinds of shells hermit crabs like the best. So biologist Brian Hazlett set up an experiment at the Duke University Marine Laboratory, in Beaufort, North Carolina.

First, Brian found some empty snail shells that looked like good crab houses. Then he collected about 50 crabs. He put the empty shells and the crabs onto a giant water table in his lab. Then he watched. Some of the crabs went to the empty shells and claimed them.

Brian examined and measured the crabs and their old and new shells. He wanted to understand why the crabs chose new shells. Brian found that the crab was looking for a shell that was not too tight or too loose. The crab chose a shell that fit just right!

Trading

Next, Brian wanted to figure out how hermit crabs find new shells. The problem is that most shells are already in use. Other crabs live in them. To get a new shell, one crab has to take another crab's shell.

What do crabs do? Do they fight for a new shell? Or do they have other ways to make an exchange?

To answer these questions, Brian set up a second experiment. He knew that crabs tap on the shell of another crab before an exchange takes place. What does the tapping mean? Is it a way to scare another crab?

Both crabs now live in more comfortable shells.

Or is it a way that hermit crabs communicate with each other?

Brian observed a total of 114 crabs. He counted the number of times crabs tapped other crabs' shells. He observed whether one crab appeared to be attacking another. He also noticed whether both crabs gained a better shell as a result of the exchange.

What Happened?

Brian observed 69 interactions between crabs. During all those interactions, tapping was involved. He found that 24 exchanges took place among the crabs. All these exchanges had a couple of things in common:

✗ A high number of taps meant that the crab really wanted the new shell.

✗ Exchanges took place when both crabs ended up with a better shell.

After reviewing these results, Brian came up with some fascinating conclusions. Hermit crabs can judge the size of a new shell. They can use this information to find the best shell for themselves.

Brian was not expecting these results.

It turns out that hermit crabs are pretty complicated creatures. ■

PART 2 CONCLUSION
Animal Behavior

GOOD TO KNOW! Cats and dogs can communicate through their postures, facial expressions, and scents.

THAT'S A FACT! Hermit crabs tap the shell of another crab a great number of times when they really want to take over its shell.

I KNOW THAT ONE! What can we learn from tracks and animal droppings?

WHAT DO YOU THINK? How do animals you know communicate their needs and feelings?

PART 3

Keeping Animals Safe

A golden lion tamarin in captivity

Some types of animals are starting to disappear from the wild. Then people have to get involved. They step in and try to help. Sometimes they can help by taking care of animals in zoos or by helping animals return to their original homes. In some cases, scientists don't know why the animals are disappearing. In those cases, they continue to study and to try to figure out what is causing the problem.

A biologist looks for frogs.

The three stories in this section include the following:

- **Animal Keeper**
- **What Happened to the Frogs?**
- **Going Home Again**

They explore how scientists work to keep animals safe. You'll find out about an animal keeper and a program that trains animals to survive in their original home. You'll also read a sad story about frogs that scientists are still struggling to help.

Animal Keeper

Roger Rosscoe is holding a baby reptile called a Komodo dragon. This creature is the world's biggest lizard.

Have you read the story in this book called "Frogs, Toads, and Other Amphibians"? If so, you may find this story especially interesting. It's about a man who takes care of amphibians and other animals for a living.

THIS IS ROGER ROSSCOE. He's an animal keeper at the Smithsonian's National Zoological Park in Washington, D.C. In addition to caring for amphibians, Roger also cares for reptiles. Reptiles have scaly skin and lay eggs that have leathery shells. Snakes and turtles are examples of reptiles. ▸

Roger's job is to make sure the animals have enough to eat and live in a safe place. "Amphibians eat crickets and other insects," Roger says. "And their water must be very clean."

Everything that touches the animals must be clean—including Roger's hands. He washes his hands often throughout the day.

Roger's day begins with a "walk-around." Can you guess what that term means? Roger "walks around" and checks every animal and the place where it lives. He keeps his eyes open for unusual behavior. If he spots a frog sitting in a pool of water, he knows something's up. She may be about to lay her eggs.

If all is well, Roger starts other chores. He redesigns a cage. He observes how many eggs a mother salamander laid. Or he watches how amphibians raise their young. He's always thinking of how he can make the animals more comfortable in the zoo.

Always an Animal Lover

Roger's always been interested in animals. When he was a kid in Long Island, New York, he went for walks in the woods with his father. They looked at insects and other creatures. Sometimes his father would catch grasshoppers and feed them to spiders.

At home, the family kept tanks of fish. But Roger's passion was salamanders. He found some in the woods and brought them home. He set them up in tanks. He also read as much as he could about salamanders. He liked one book a lot. It's called *Salamanders of New York*, by Sherman Bishop. Roger couldn't put the book down.

Roger Rosscoe had a passion for salamanders like this one.

Roger continued to collect, keep, and observe salamanders. He tried to learn as much about them as he could. Later, Roger went to college to learn more about animals. A few years after Roger finished college, he started working at the National Zoo.

Keeping Animals Safe

The Reptile Discovery Center at the National Zoo

In his part of the Reptile Discovery Center, where the amphibians live, Roger works with seven kinds of frogs and four kinds of salamanders.

Something New Every Day

Roger likes his job very much. Each day is a little different. In his part of the Reptile Discovery Center, where the amphibians live, Roger works with seven kinds of frogs and four kinds of salamanders. "They all have different habits," he says. "I have done lots of reading on these animals, but just being able to see them every day is great," he says.

"The people I work with are great, too," Roger continues. "They all have a passion for the animals." Roger says his job is ideal. "I can't see myself doing anything else."

ANIMAL STUDIES • STC BOOKS

What Happened to the Frogs?

August 1995. Some middle school students were on a field trip to a pond in Minnesota. Their plan was to study the animals and plants there. They were not prepared for what they saw that day.

It was the frogs. About half of them had serious problems. Some frogs were missing legs. Others had oddly shaped legs. Still others had extra legs. The students were sad to see the frogs looking this way.

About a year later, other people noticed frogs with big problems in many other places in Minnesota. Then the deformed frogs showed up in other states. Something strange was going on.

Collecting Data

Frogs like these had never been seen so often before. Scientists were worried. They thought that the water had materials in it that were bad for the frogs. Or maybe a new disease was attacking the frogs. Scientists weren't sure. So they set up an experiment.

First, researchers collected water samples from places in Minnesota where deformed frogs were found. Then they collected water from places where healthy frogs lived.

Here's what a healthy frog looks like.

Here's one of the frogs they observed in Minnesota.

Keeping Animals Safe

A biologist uses a net to collect frogs.

Next, researchers collected eggs from healthy frogs. They placed some eggs in water where deformed frogs had been found. They placed other eggs in water where healthy frogs had been found.

Their Findings

What do you think happened? What kinds of frogs developed in the water where deformed frogs had been found? What kinds of frogs developed where healthy frogs had been found?

Here's what scientists discovered:

- The frogs raised in the water where deformed frogs had been found had problems similar to those the Minnesota frogs had.

- The frogs raised in the water where healthy frogs had been found were fine.

Still Working

Now scientists knew that something was wrong with the water. But they didn't know what. They're still working on this problem. They hope to solve this mystery very soon.

Learning about frogs is important.

What's hurting their habitat may be hurting ours, too. So scientists are interested in finding out as much as they can.

ANIMAL STUDIES • STC BOOKS   39

going Home again

JESSIE COHEN, NATIONAL ZOOLOGICAL PARK, SMITHSONIAN INSTITUTION

Standing on its hind legs, a golden lion tamarin looks for food. It sees some sitting on a leaf and is ready to grab it. Do you think the tamarin is in its natural environment? Well, think again. The tamarin, a kind of monkey, lives in the Smithsonian Institution's National Zoological Park in Washington, D.C.

Why are zookeepers hiding the tamarin's food? The reason is that the Zoo's tamarins are being trained to survive in their original home, in the forests of Brazil.

An Animal at Risk

The story of the golden lion tamarins began many years ago. The tamarins lived in the tropical forests of Brazil. They had enough food to eat. They produced enough baby tamarins. All was well until about 200 years ago.

Then the forest began to change. Settlers moved in. They began clearing the forests for farms, plantations, and pastures. Without the trees, the tamarins didn't know how to survive. They began

Keeping Animals Safe

to die out. In 1970, only about 500 tamarins were left in the forests of Brazil.

Tamarins also lived in zoos around the world. But they weren't doing very well in the zoos either. Zoo tamarins had trouble producing babies. So scientists worked very hard to change their living areas. They wanted to make sure the tamarins were as comfortable as possible.

Their efforts paid off. The number of tamarins born in zoos began to rise. By 1981, about 400 golden tamarins were living in zoos.

Bringing Tamarins Home

Scientists were pleased that the tamarins were doing better in zoos. But the scientists still weren't satisfied. They wanted to try an experiment. They wanted to bring the animals home to Brazil.

It was a good time to try this experiment. Farmers and ranchers had given back some of the land. New forests had been planted. Now there was a place for the tamarins.

But first, the tamarins had to be trained to live in the forest. Zoo workers were in charge of their training. It went on for several months. As you already saw, zoo workers hid the tamarins' food. The tamarins had to search for it.

Zoo workers also changed their living area. They made it more like a forest. They hung branches, ropes, and vines in the zoo. The tamarins had to learn how to travel on ropes to move from tree to tree. The keepers changed the ropes often. Then the animals had to figure out new ways to get around.

Golden lion tamarins in the zoo

ANIMAL STUDIES • STC BOOKS   41

Golden lion tamarins play in a tree.

Some tamarins were even moved to woods in the zoo. There they could live freely on their own. All this was good practice for Brazil.

Other Challenges

The researchers had other concerns. One was disease. Researchers feared that tamarins raised in zoos might carry new diseases to the tamarins in Brazil. If that happened, the wild animals could be destroyed.

The solution, the scientists decided, was quarantine. That means that the zoo tamarins were separated from the wild ones for a period of time—about 30 days. Then veterinarians examined the tamarins very carefully. If the vets said that the tamarins were healthy, they could be taken back to the forests of Brazil.

Scientists also worried about how the zoo tamarins would get along with those in the wild. Would the zoo tamarins attack the wild ones? Would they try to take their mates and young? The scientists decided not to take any chances. They searched for forests that didn't have any tamarins. They found some new forests that had been donated by Brazilian ranchers. The researchers decided to put the zoo tamarins there.

What Happened to the Tamarins?

Year after year, researchers brought small groups of zoo tamarins to Brazil. Over time, 153 made the journey. Many survived. New tamarins were born in the forest. They did very well. Curious and quick learners, they easily learned how to find food and travel around the forest.

Moving tamarins back to Brazil has been a success.

Today about 460 more tamarins live in the forests of Brazil than were there 30 years ago.

PART 3 CONCLUSION
Keeping Animals Safe

THAT'S A FACT!   Animal keepers are responsible for making sure that animals in zoos have enough food and water, have a comfortable place to live, and are caring for their young.

I KNOW THAT ONE!   Why did golden lion tamarins almost die out? What did scientists do to help them?

WHAT DO YOU THINK?   Why were some of the frogs in Minnesota deformed?

SCIENTISTS AT WORK

PART 4

Scientists at Work

This section includes the following five stories:
- **The Amazing Discoveries of Charles Darwin**
- **Jean-Henri Fabré: Science Pioneer**
- **Orangutans and How They Learn**
- **The Story of Konrad Lorenz**
- **Jane Goodall and Her Life with the Chimps**

Scientists like these have been studying animals for many years. They have observed how the animals survive in their own environments. In this section, you'll meet the scientist who first used this approach.

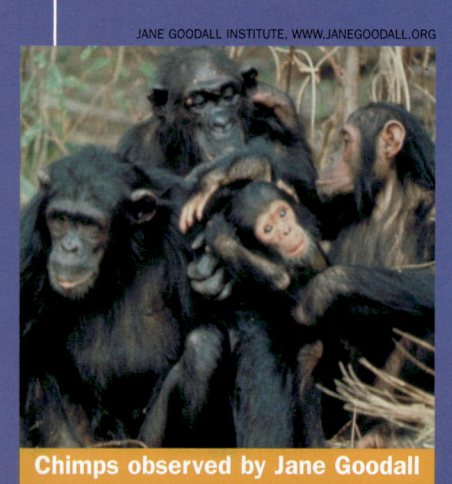

More recently, other scientists have studied our closest relatives, the apes. They have discovered how advanced these animals are and how much they can learn.

An iguana on the Galápagos Islands

Chimps observed by Jane Goodall

Butterflies were one of many insects that Jean-Henri Fabré studied.

Scientists at Work

The Amazing Discoveries of *Charles Darwin*

Have you ever heard of Charles Darwin? He was a kind of scientist called a naturalist. A naturalist studies plants, animals, rocks, and soil—everything that is part of nature. Darwin traveled to places where he saw plants and animals that no scientists had ever seen before. Based on what he saw, he came up with a new and exciting theory about the natural world. A theory is an explanation of why things are the way they are.

But we are getting ahead of ourselves. In 1825, long before he became famous, Darwin was a teenager growing up in England. He loved the outdoors. He enjoyed fishing, hunting, and exploring the English countryside. He collected plants, insects, and birds' eggs.

Discovering a Passion

Like many of you, Charles didn't know what he wanted to be when he grew up. But his father had an idea. He wanted Charles to be a doctor. He was a doctor, and so was Charles's grandfather. Charles's father thought that medicine was the right job for his son.

Charles went to medical school but he didn't like it at all. Classes put him to sleep. He really hated seeing people suffer. He knew he would not be a good doctor.

His father agreed. "How would you like to become a minister?" he suggested. "Not much," thought Charles. "But maybe I would have time to add to my science collection."

Charles went to Cambridge University to study religion. He ▸

ANIMAL STUDIES ● STC BOOKS   **45**

Young Charles Darwin

didn't enjoy his classes, but he liked the university. He became friends with two scientists—John Stevens Henslow and Adam Sedgewick. Dr. Henslow was a botanist, a scientist who studies plants. Dr. Sedgewick was a geologist, a scientist who studies rocks and fossils. They invited Charles on field trips and long nature walks. They collected plants and rocks. Charles learned a lot about nature.

In 1831, Charles graduated from Cambridge. He was 23 years old. He wasn't sure what he was going to do. One day, a letter from Dr. Henslow arrived. He had recommended Charles for a job aboard a British ship called the *Beagle*. The ship was traveling around the world. Charles's job was to do what he liked best—collect plants and animals. The job was a perfect fit. Charles was very excited.

The *Beagle* Sails

The *Beagle* set sail on December 27, 1831. The first weeks of the voyage were discouraging. Charles's cabin was tiny, and his bed was uncomfortable. He was seasick all the time. Charles wondered whether he had made a mistake.

Finally the ship made its first stop.

The *Beagle*

Charles found himself on the Cape Verde Islands. The Cape Verde Islands is a country made up of 15 islands

46 ANIMAL STUDIES • STC BOOKS

Scientists at Work

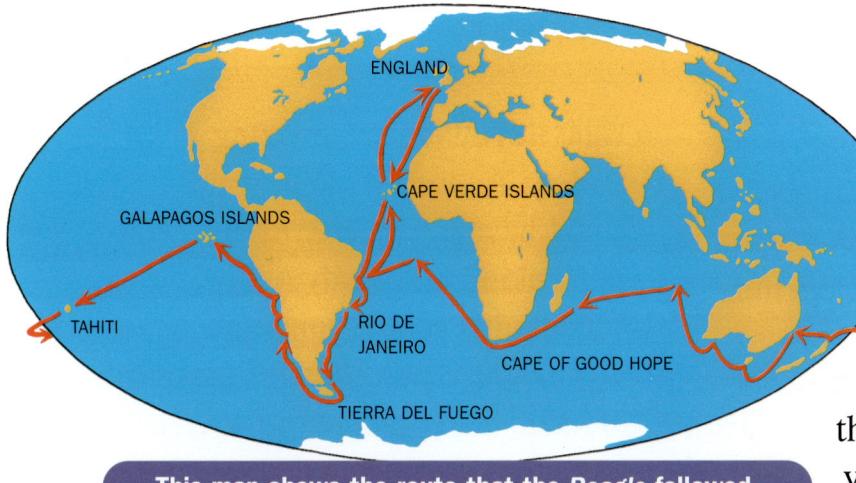

This map shows the route that the *Beagle* followed.

off the west coast of Africa. Once on land, Charles was no longer seasick. Charles was thrilled by the strange plants and animals he saw.

From then on, the trip got better and better. The *Beagle* made many stops. Charles Darwin explored the rain forests of Brazil and the plains of Argentina. But no place was more exciting than the islands of the Galápagos. The Galápagos are located about 960 kilometers (600 miles) west of South America.

Charles spent five weeks exploring the Galápagos. He saw two different kinds of giant turtles and two forms of lizards, known as iguanas. He also saw a number of different types of birds. Charles was amazed by how unique each animal was. He wondered how such different creatures had developed.

As Charles explored the islands, he wrote pages and pages of notes. He collected fossils, butterflies, spiders, crabs, plants, and skins of birds. He shipped box after box of samples back to England.

In November 1835, the *Beagle* reached Tahiti. A year later, October 2, 1836, the ship landed back in England. Charles had been traveling for almost five years.

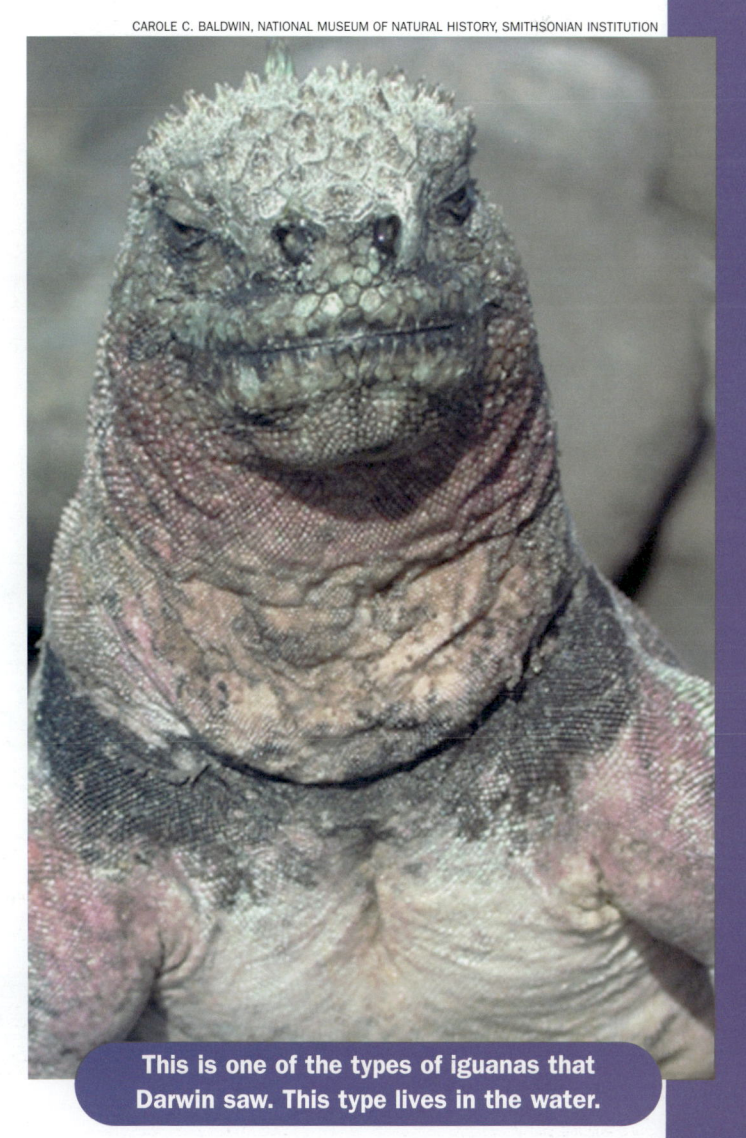

CAROLE C. BALDWIN, NATIONAL MUSEUM OF NATURAL HISTORY, SMITHSONIAN INSTITUTION

This is one of the types of iguanas that Darwin saw. This type lives in the water.

ANIMAL STUDIES • STC BOOKS   47

After the Voyage

The voyage was over, but Charles had much work to do. He and other scientists described the samples from the Galápagos. Then Charles wrote a book about his travels. He called the book *The Voyage of the Beagle*. The book was published in 1839. It was an instant success.

The trip had changed Charles's life. He couldn't put out of his mind what he had seen. His experiences raised many questions about life on Earth. He wondered where different kinds of plants and animals came from. He thought about why living things change from generation to generation. Over time, he developed an important theory about plants and animals. His theory explained how new kinds of animals and plants develop. This process is called evolution.

Here's a brief summary of Charles Darwin's amazing ideas.

- **DARWIN OBSERVED** plants and animals on isolated islands. They didn't have contact with plants and animals from anywhere else. Darwin's first thought was that all the plants and animals should look the same.

- **WHAT HE FOUND** was amazing variety. He wondered how this could have happened. After years of thinking and studying, he came to his conclusion: animals do change. Some changes make animals better suited to their environment, while others do not. The animals that survive are those with the changes that make them better suited to their environment. This is the process that Darwin called natural selection.

- **NATURAL SELECTION** takes place all the time. Over long periods of time, natural selection results in adaptations. You have read about many different adaptations in this book. Adaptations are physical characteristics and behaviors that make it possible for animals to survive in their environment.

Darwin's theory changed the way people looked at the world. They began to understand that nothing stays exactly the same. The world and all the animals that live in it are changing all the time. They are still changing, even today.

Scientists at Work

The submersible called the *Johnson Sea Link II* and scientists preparing to explore the underwater world of the Galápagos.

A Visit to the Galápagos

IN 1998, scientists Carole Baldwin and David Pawson from the Smithsonian Institution's National Museum of Natural History and John McCosker from the California Academy of Sciences went to the Galápagos Islands. They had two main goals. One was to make a movie for the Smithsonian called *Galápagos*. The second goal of the trip was to explore the islands. These scientists had tools that Charles Darwin never dreamed of. With scuba gear and an underwater vehicle called a submersible, they could explore the ocean. The submersible could go as deep as 3,000 meters (9,840 feet).

Their trip was a success. The movie was made for a very, very big screen. If you put on special glasses, the creatures seem like they are right in front of you. Pretty amazing!

The scientists also made some new discoveries. Just as Charles Darwin found new animals on land, these scientists saw new animals in the water. The animals shown on this page are some examples of the creatures that these scientists discovered. ■

A new kind of starfish

A new kind of sea urchin

ANIMAL STUDIES ● STC BOOKS 49

Jean-Henri Fabré:

Jean-Henri Fabré

Science Pioneer

A man leans over a spider web. He is using a magnifier to watch a spider. He is wearing a big black hat and smoking a pipe. Who is this man, and what do you think he is doing?

His name was Jean-Henri Fabré. He was a scientist who lived in France in the 1800s. Believe it or not, Jean-Henri was doing something very unique for his time. He was studying an animal in its own environment.

Back then, scientists liked to study animals in their labs. Or, they would go to farms to observe sheep or cattle. No one thought to study animals where they lived—until Jean-Henri came along.

50 ANIMAL STUDIES • STC BOOKS

Scientists at Work

Now it's your turn. Take a look at this spider web. How would you describe it?

At Home on the Farm

Jean-Henri liked to share his love of animals with other people, so he became a teacher. He wrote many books about insects and another major interest—mushrooms. What Jean-Henri liked best, though, was observing animals. He didn't have much money, but in 1879, Jean-Henri bought a small farm. There he spent his free time looking at insects and spiders. He observed them up close with a magnifier. He measured the animals with his ruler. He wrote down what he saw in his notebook.

Jean-Henri was very good at drawing and painting watercolors. He created beautiful images of the animals and plants he observed.

Observing Spiders

Jean-Henri loved spiders most of all. He was fascinated with how they spun their webs. He was one of the first scientists to watch spiders at work. He wrote down how they wove their delicate webs. Jean-Henri described patterns of webs for several different kinds of spiders. Here's one observation from his notebook:

"A special thread, the foundation of the real net, stretched across the area . . . the post that will quiet and bring order into the wilderness of twists and turns."

Does his description remind you of a spider web? In addition to being a scientist, Jean-Henri was also a poet. He used his imagination to write his descriptions of animals. That's why he's also known as the "Poet of Science."

Working Alone

Jean-Henri knew some other scientists from the university, but he usually worked alone. As he got older, his work was ▶

ANIMAL STUDIES ● STC BOOKS 51

> "A special thread, the foundation of the real net, stretched across the area . . . the post that will quiet and bring order into the wilderness of twists and turns."

admired by some famous scientists, including Charles Darwin and Louis Pasteur, who came to see Jean-Henri on his farm. Jean-Henri even received a prize from the ruler of France—Napoleon the Third. Jean-Henri died in 1915, at age 92.

Rediscovered

Nearly 50 years after Jean-Henri died, a group of scientists studied his notebooks. They were amazed at how much he had learned. The scientists wondered whether Jean-Henri's methods were better than their own.

The scientists decided to use Jean-Henri's pioneering approach. They used his methods to study many different animals. They went to the ocean to study crabs. They sloshed around in marshes to study frogs.

Today, scientists don't think it's unusual to study animals in their own environment. They have learned a lot by living with animals. In fact, they probably think it's strange *not* to go where the animals are.

Jean-Henri Fabré was a real pioneer. He changed the way scientists everywhere study animals. ■

From top: Stag beetle, Bess bug, Monarch butterfly

Scientists at Work

Orangutans
and How They Learn

Orangutans at the Smithsonian Institution's National Zoological Park lead an interesting life. They do a lot more than eat, sleep, and move around.

Researcher Robert Shumaker built them a unique place to live. It's called the Think Tank. Here scientists study how orangutans and other animals think.

The Think Tank is one of the zoo's many exhibits. As orangutans learn, visitors can watch them at work. That is really cool. Who knows? Maybe you'll be there when the orangutans learn something new! ▸

ANIMAL STUDIES • STC BOOKS 53

> They have learned to use symbols that stand for the names of foods, objects, action words, and numbers.

What do you think this orangutan, an adult male named Azy, is pointing to?

❶

A grape! It is one of Azy's favorite foods.

Picking Out the Right Symbol

One of Robert's experiments was to see if orangutans can learn a language. He taught the orangutans a language of symbols made from different shapes. For example, the symbol name for grapes is a rectangle with a diagonal line inside it. Robert invented the language. Robert found that the orangutans could learn it. They learned to use symbols that stand for the names of foods, objects, action words, and numbers. The orangutans worked their way through a dictionary of 70 symbols.

Here's how Robert taught the orangutans:

❶ First, Robert showed the orangutan what it was supposed to name and the symbol for it. Second, the orangutan looked at the computer screen and made a choice. When a symbol was new, there might be only the right answer and a wrong answer on the computer screen. Once the orangutan understood how to use the symbol, the screens could be more complicated. These apes could find the right answer on screens that had 28 different symbols!

Scientists at Work

JESSIE COHEN, NATIONAL ZOOLOGICAL PARK, SMITHSONIAN INSTITUTION

2 Azy did a good job. So Robert gives him the grape that he named correctly.

3 Now Azy is happy!

The Orangutan Language Project continues at the National Zoo.

Robert Shumaker moved to the Great Ape Trust of Iowa, to continue his study of orangutans there. He now has more than 20 years of experience studying what he once called "these awesome creatures." ■

ANIMAL STUDIES ● STC BOOKS   55

The Story of Konrad Lorenz

The geese with Konrad Lorenz

HONK! HONK!

Konrad Lorenz was a famous scientist. He lived in Vienna, Austria, most of his life, from 1903 to 1989. During his long life, he studied fish, ducks, geese, and other animals. He watched animals very closely. He was able to learn a great deal. In fact, he was one of the first scientists to figure out how animals learn.

Lorenz was especially interested in ducks and geese. He did many experiments with these animals. He was the first to discover one important way that ducks and geese learn.

What Did Lorenz Discover?

Konrad watched geese come out of their shells. He noticed that they started following their mother right away and followed her everywhere she went.

By chance, Lorenz noticed that if young geese didn't see their mother after hatching, they acted differently. They didn't follow their mother around. They didn't do what the other geese did.

Lorenz wondered what this meant. "Geese must need to see something right away," he thought. "But does it have to be their mother? What would happen if they saw me first?"

Lorenz set up an experiment to find out. First, he found some eggs that were just about ready to hatch. When the birds were coming out, he moved the mother out of the way. He stood in her place. Konrad was the first thing the geese saw. He also moved around and made honking sounds. What do you think happened?

Believe it or not, the geese started following him. They may have thought Lorenz was their mother. He took care of them for the rest of their lives. When the geese grew up, the males wanted him to be their mate. They preferred him over the other geese! Isn't that fascinating?

Next, Konrad tried the experiment with ducks. He found that ducks were like geese. They also followed human beings. Ducks would even follow objects, such as moving balls, as if the balls were their mother.

A Major Discovery

Lorenz had just made an important discovery. Geese and ducks would follow the first moving object they saw after hatching. Konrad called this finding *imprinting*. That's because the behavior was imprinted into the bird at a very early age. Once the behavior was there, it would never go away.

Lorenz made this discovery in the late 1930s. Almost 40 years later, he was honored by his fellow scientists. In 1973, he won the Nobel Prize for his work with ducks and geese. Today, he is considered a pioneer in ethology, the study of animal behavior.

Jane Goodall and Her Life with the Chimps

PART 1:
Jane Goodall Discovers Science

What do you want to be when you grow up? Do you dream about writing a novel or traveling to the moon?

Back in the 1930s, a young woman named Jane Goodall had a dream. She wanted to study animals. Her dream came true. She became one of the first women to study a group of chimpanzees that lived in a country in Africa called Tanzania.

Jane on the Peak

Atlantic Ocean

MIDDLE EAST

AFRICA

Tanzania

Here's where Tanzania is located.

Here's her story...

Jane Loved Animals

Jane was born in England in 1934. As a child, she loved being around animals. Her family lived in a house in the country. She helped take care of geese, hens, and cows. She also learned how to ride horses. Many days, she and her friends went on long walks in the woods. They observed different animals. When they came home, they tried to find out more about these animals in books. Jane was always curious.

In the winter, Jane would curl up in front of the fireplace reading her favorite books—*Tarzan*, the *Jungle Book*, and *Dr. Doolittle*. "I think that was when I first decided I must go to Africa someday," Jane recalls.

Following Her Dream

When Jane was 21 years old, she visited Africa. There she met a scientist named Louis Leakey. He was interested in animals, too. He talked with Jane about her future. He was very impressed with how much she knew about African animals. Jane told him that she wanted to learn even more. "I want to come as close to talking to animals as I can and move among them without fear," she told Leakey.

It just so happened that Leakey was looking for someone to study a group of chimpanzees that lived near a lake in Tanzania. After talking to Jane, Leakey realized that he had found the right person.

Jane Goodall with Louis Leakey

Her Dream Comes True

Jane set off for Africa in 1960. She was 26 years old. She and a few other people made camp in a lovely spot near a small, fast-flowing stream. Her day began at 5:30 in the morning. After breakfast, she climbed to a high place, known as the Peak, to look for the chimpanzees.

First, she would watch the chimps through her binoculars. One of the first things she discovered was that most of the time, chimps wandered

Members of the chimp community that Jane studied

about in small groups. Often, she saw a mother with her children or two or three adult males by themselves.

When feeding on ripe fruit, many groups would join together and make a lot of noise! Jane realized that she was watching one large community of about 50 chimps.

After the chimps finished eating, Jane would collect some of the leaves, flowers, or fruits they left behind. She wanted to see what they had been eating. She discovered that the chimps ate mostly fruits. They also ate many different kinds of leaves, blossoms, seeds, and stems. Later, she found out that they ate insects, too. Sometimes the chimps hunted for meat.

At Home on the Peak

Jane spent many, many hours on the Peak. She kept a blanket with her and slept on the Peak near the chimps. She learned that chimps sleep all night, just as we do. Mothers and young chimps sleep together in a nest. She watched them build their nest by bending branches down, one over the other. Then they made a soft pillow out of lots of small, soft leafy twigs.

Although Jane spent so much time near the chimps, they still didn't let her get near them. But Jane was patient. She was willing to wait until they were ready.

PART 2: Living with the Chimps

Jane had to wait a long time until the chimps trusted her. Finally, her luck changed. Her big break came in the form of a large male chimp. Jane called him David Greybeard.

One evening, after returning to camp, Jane received the news that a large chimp had wandered nearby. Jane was ecstatic!

The next day, Jane waited for the chimp the whole day. Late in the afternoon, he arrived. David Greybeard ate the nuts growing on the palm tree. He nibbled on the bananas Jane had put out for him. The meeting was the beginning of a friendship.

Jane spent many, many hours on the Peak. She kept a blanket with her and slept on the Peak near the chimps.

Jane made one of her most exciting discoveries while observing David Greybeard. First, he picked up a blade of grass and poked it into a termite mound. When he pulled the grass out, it was covered with termites. Termites are small insects. He put the grass in his mouth and ate the termites. Then he picked up a little twig, stripped off the leaves, and used it to get more termites.

Jane had just observed David using objects as tools. He also had made a tool. Before this observation, scientists had thought that only humans could make tools.

Back at Camp

Every evening, Jane returned to camp for dinner. Then she would write her observations in her journal. Jane always said how important it was to write in her journal immediately. That way, her observations were still fresh in her mind.

Slowly, Jane began to recognize more of the chimps as individuals. She gave them all names. She named one chimpanzee Flo. "She was easy to pick out," Jane said. "She had a big nose and ragged ears." Flo would come to camp with her infant daughter. Jane named the baby Fifi.

Jane soon learned that female chimps in Africa have only one baby every five or six years. She also saw how all the family members helped one another.

The Jane Goodall Institute

Jane spent many years living with chimpanzees and studying them. She watched baby chimpanzees learn how to communicate using gestures much like our own—holding hands, kissing, and patting each other.

Today, Jane travels around the world, talking to people about her discoveries. In 1975, she established The Jane Goodall Institute for Wildlife Research, Education and Conservation. The organization promotes research and education about animals and their humane treatment.

Jane has spent her life protecting chimpanzees and other animals. She continues to travel around the world, telling people everywhere about her fascinating experiences.

PART 4 CONCLUSION
Scientists at Work

THAT'S A FACT! Charles Darwin's theory of natural selection changed the way people looked at the world. The theory helped many people realize that nothing stays exactly the same.

DID YOU KNOW THAT... . . . Jean-Henri Fabré was the first scientist to observe animals in their natural environment?

WHAT DO YOU THINK? What did Jane Goodall learn about chimps in Africa?

COOL FACT! Konrad Lorenz discovered one way geese and ducks learn—through imprinting.

Glossary

ADAPTATION: A body structure or behavior that enables an animal to better survive or to reproduce in its environment; the process by which an organism changes.

AMPHIBIAN: A group of cold-blooded animals with backbones; most of them spend their early life in the water and most of their adult life on land. Frogs, toads, and salamanders are amphibians.

BOTANIST: A scientist who studies plants.

COLD-BLOODED: Animals without a constant body temperature; their temperature is dependent on their environment.

CRUSTACEAN: A class of animals with outside skeletons, jointed bodies, and limbs. They have gills and live mostly in the water. Crabs and lobsters are examples of crustaceans.

ECOLOGIST: A scientist who studies how living things interact with each other and their environment.

ENVIRONMENT: Everything that surrounds an organism and influences it.

ETHOLOGY: The scientific study of animal behavior.

EXPERIMENT: A procedure that is carried out to investigate a scientific question.

GEOLOGIST: A scientist who studies rocks, rock formations, and fossils.

HABITAT: The place where plants and animals naturally live.

IMPRINTING: The way in which animals such as ducks and geese learn by following a model or a pattern; for example, a hatching goose follows the first moving object it sees.

MAMMAL: Animals that are warm-blooded, have hair or fur on their bodies, and can be fed milk from their mother's bodies.

METAMORPHOSIS: A change in form or structure. Word used to describe the stages that some animals undergo during their life cycle.

MIGRATION: The regular, seasonal trip animals take from one place to another to find food or shelter, or to produce their young.

NATURALIST: A scientist who studies the natural world.

NATURAL SELECTION: The process through which living things best suited to their environment survive and produce young.

OBSERVATION: Information that an individual receives by using his or her senses to closely study something; for example, the behavior of an animal in its environment. Observations are the first step in learning about something new.

PREDATOR: An animal that feeds on other animals; a predator is adapted to capture its prey.

PREY: An animal hunted by a predator for food.

REPTILE: A group of cold-blooded animals that have scaly skin and lay eggs with leathery shells.

STRUCTURE: The way in which the parts of an object or living thing are arranged.

THEORY: An explanation, based on observations and experiments, that explains why things are the way they are. For example, natural selection is a theory that explains why animals change over time.

WARM-BLOODED: Animals that produce heat in their bodies and maintain a constant body temperature.

ZOOLOGIST: A scientist who studies animals.

ANIMAL STUDIES • STC BOOKS

photo credits

COVER (from top left, clockwise) Jessie Cohen, National Zoological Park, Smithsonian Institution; Courtesy of Carolina Biological Supply Company; Jessie Cohen, National Zoological Park, Smithsonian Institution; Jessie Cohen, National Zoological Park, Smithsonian Institution

TITLE PAGE Jessie Cohen, National Zoological Park, Smithsonian Institution

PAGE 3 (from top) Courtesy of Minnesota Pollution Control Agency, St. Paul, MN; Courtesy of Carolina Biological Supply Company

5 (from top) Courtesy of Carolina Biological Supply Company; Smithsonian Environmental Research Center

6 (from top) Jessie Cohen, National Zoological Park, Smithsonian Institution; Courtesy of Carolina Biological Supply Company

7 (both) Courtesy of Carolina Biological Supply Company

9 Courtesy of Brenda Davis, Maryland Department of Natural Resources

10 (both) Smithsonian Environmental Research Center

12 Jessie Cohen, National Zoological Park, Smithsonian Institution

13 Smithsonian Environmental Research Center

14 Smithsonian Environmental Research Center

15 NSRC

16 Courtesy of Stephanie Elliott Garnett

17 Courtesy of Carolina Biological Supply Company

27 Courtesy of Phil Jones

30 Jessie Cohen, National Zoological Park, Smithsonian Institution

34 (from top) Jessie Cohen, National Zoological Park, Smithsonian Institution; Courtesy of Minnesota Pollution Control Agency, St. Paul, MN

35 Jessie Cohen, National Zoological Park, Smithsonian Institution

36 Royalty free

37 Jessie Cohen, National Zoological Park, Smithsonian Institution

38 (from left) Courtesy of Roy W. McDiarmid; Courtesy of Minnesota Pollution Control Agency, St. Paul, MN

39 Courtesy of Minnesota Pollution Control Agency, St. Paul, MN

40 Jessie Cohen, National Zoological Park, Smithsonian Institution

41 Jessie Cohen, National Zoological Park, Smithsonian Institution

42 Jessie Cohen, National Zoological Park, Smithsonian Institution

44 (clockwise from top) Carole C. Baldwin, National Museum of Natural History, Smithsonian Institution; Courtesy of Carolina Biological Supply Company; Jane Goodall Institute, www.janegoodall.org

46 Smithsonian Institution Archives, Record Unit 95, Photograph Collection, Neg.# 45892

47 Carole C. Baldwin, National Museum of Natural History, Smithsonian Institution

49 (top) Carole C. Baldwin, National Museum of Natural History, Smithsonian Institution; (bottom two) Dave Pawson, National Museum of Natural History, Smithsonian Institution

51 Courtesy of Carolina Biological Supply Company

52 (all) Courtesy of Carolina Biological Supply Company

53 Jessie Cohen, National Zoological Park, Smithsonian Institution

54 Jessie Cohen, National Zoological Park, Smithsonian Institution

55 (both) Jessie Cohen, National Zoological Park, Smithsonian Institution

56 Private Donor

58 Jane Goodall Institute, www.janegoodall.org

59 Jane Goodall Institute, www.janegoodall.org

60 Jane Goodall Institute, www.janegoodall.org